UPWARDS

10 Essential Leadership Lessons to Advance your Career and Improve Your Life

TABITHA HAPEMAN

This is dedicated to my family, who have tirelessly supported me on my journey and made writing this book possible.

CONTENTS

UPWARDS

I didn't bring enough water. That's a terrifying thought; it's almost as if electroactivity is sparking through my body as those words float through my mind. The trail marker is the halfway point, or just before the halfway point. My rain jacket is not doing anything to prevent me from being soaked through. Between the relentless rain, humidity, and how much I'm sweating, I'm completely water-logged.

There is an undeniable irony in being soaked and in the middle of a downpour the moment I realize I don't have enough water. Fleeting thoughts of building a rain catchment system with my jacket or finding a smooth rock I can use to funnel water into my near empty bottle, flit through my mind at the speed of light. Those are ridiculous thoughts, which my conscious mind knows full well.

The thought that I am relentlessly turning over like an emotional support Rubik's cube is whether to turn back. The trail behind me is a skinny river of mud, as my soaked feet can attest. I chose this trail because the view from the top of the mountain is supposed to be incredible. The description online called it "panoramic."

If I turn back now, a little before the halfway point, I will only see the same parts of the trail I've already seen. The way back, however, is mostly downhill. If I keep going forward, I will reach the summit and hopefully experience the amazing view I've read about. Either way, I'll be out of water, wet, and thirsty. Whether I turn back or keep climbing upwards on the trail, I will be uncomfortable.

With a dry mouth and wet socks, I turn towards the bend that will take me upwards to the summit. Four more miles to go until I'm back at my car. Another mile until I reach the summit. I tell myself that as long as I keep moving, I should be unlikely to get hypothermic. As long as I keep moving, I'll eventually get back to the safety of my campsite.

And so, I go upwards.

Upwards

INTRODUCTION: THE BEGINNING OF THE LESSON

On my first day of freshman orientation, I found myself sitting around a conference room table with about half a dozen of my fellow students. We were all waiting to meet with Larry, our student advisor, who would see us through successfully completing our first year of our college education. The room was filled with hopeful optimism tinged with a touch of anxiety, and I sat quietly listening to the small talk happening around me. At 18 years old, I was not a social butterfly and preferred to observe rather than engage.

The conversation shifted to what specialty or field of nursing everyone was planning to pursue when they graduated. Graduation was four years away, but nearly all of us seemed to have an idea of where we wanted to go with our careers, and there wasn't any doubt in anyone's mind they would successfully complete their degree. The joys and optimism of youth!

One person shared that her grandfather was a cancer survivor, and the nurses who cared for him were so amazing that she was inspired to pursue nursing and specialize in oncology. Another person said she loved babies and wanted to work in labor and delivery. I think someone mentioned sports medicine or orthopedics at some point. Then, the round robin style conversation found its way to me.

Having all eyes on me wasn't as comfortable a situation as it is now. Now, I love being in front of a crowd and speaking on what I'm passionate about. Back then, however, I was awkward when attention was focused on me unless I had prepared ahead of time. Compounding my discomfort was the fact that I didn't know what I wanted to do with my career. I had a desire I didn't know how to articulate and a goal that wasn't as clear cut as my peers.

The summer before I started school, my sister and I would walk with a friend on the dike along the Susquehanna River. We'd met our friend Maria through church, and she was older than us and more seasoned in life. She was already engaged to be married and had graduated college, while I was just entering that season of life and my sister was still in high school.

As we were walking, Maria asked me what I wanted to do in life. She didn't mean from a philosophical or metaphysical perspective. Like most Americans, when she asked, "what do you want to do," she was asking what kind of work I was going to pursue. At that point, I hadn't applied to the nursing program of my college. I was slated to start school as a communications major.

I knew I wanted to make a difference in some meaningful way, but I didn't how to go about that. I was also scared of entering nursing school, as I didn't know how to bridge my concept of a floor nurse and my wider desires. As a young woman with vague dreams of making a lasting positive impact on the world, I thought nursing was too limiting – I was very wrong, by the way!

I turned to Maria and said, "I don't know, but I'm going to work for a Fortune 500 company."

I must admit that at the time, I wasn't sure what a Fortune 500 company was, but I knew they were important and, I assumed, prestigious. I didn't know how to communicate my desire to achieve something great in life and make a lasting impact on the world, so I phrased my goals in the best way I knew at that time.

She looked puzzled for a moment and then asked, "doing what?"

I couldn't answer her because I didn't know. As the conversation continued, she pressured me to articulate a plan and have a clearer direction. My answer was not specific enough and I think seemed to her more like a vague dream than a goal. Maria is an awesome person, and I'm not criticizing her reaction to my answer. I think a lot of people would react similarly when faced with a soon-to-be college student who seemingly lacked direction.

Since early in my childhood, I had been attracted to nursing and medicine, but I couldn't understand what my career would look like if I pursued that path. Feeling called to do something is an interesting sensation, as we don't always understand why we are drawn to something. Some people describe a calling as a deep sense of intuition or discerning what their future will hold. Others may describe it as understanding their life purpose. Whatever way you define it, it's a strong feeling.

It's also a feeling we can resist. My dad shared with me when I was young that he felt called to be in ministry. He was a young man, and his youth was not typical in any way. In his teens and young adulthood, he was not what people would have described as meek, or humble, or demure. He was tough. He was a firefighter, a young drinker, and a tradesman. When he first felt called to pivot in life and join the ministry, he railed against God. He described standing on the banks of the river and yelling towards the sky that he wasn't going to join a stuck-up, holier-than-thou religion. He did eventually join the ministry, but that's a story for another book.

I did not stand in public and rage at the sky when I decided to ignore feeling called to pursue nursing. I just quietly applied to the English program, with communications as my chosen major, despite recollecting the dozen or so times I had told my grandmother, a retired nurse, before she passed that I would be a nurse too. My rebellion was quieter, but no less stubborn that my dad's.

The entire summer before school had been characterized by my internal struggle between maintaining my choice to pursue a communications major or do as my dad suggested and switch to the nursing program. It took many tearful conversations, where my dad shared the wisdom that comes with age, and internal searching for me to accept I felt called to nursing. I had applied to the nursing program only a week before the semester began and was still a little shocked I had been accepted.

By the time I started the semester, I had an inkling that nursing, and business and leadership would somehow go together, but the exact intertwining of those things was still a mystery to me.

Those conversations came back to me as I stared at my want-to-be-nurses peers and said, "I don't know, but I want to go to work in a suit."

There were some disbelieving guffaws at that proclamation.

I will never forget one of my peers turning to me and saying, "I don't think you understand what nurses do."

I shrugged and redirected the conversation, but I thought to myself – no, *you* don't understand what nurses do. To be fair, neither did I, but I was firm in my belief that somehow my decision to pursue that degree and path was the right one. As I said, a calling is a strong feeling.

These interactions became core memories, and the foundation for a lot of lessons I've learned in my leadership career. Sometimes, people won't understand your vision. Sometimes you won't know how to align your values and goals with the stark reality of your current opportunities. Sometimes, your path will only be illuminated as you take that next step; the step beyond that will still be darkened. I am learning every day how to be a better leader and the best version of myself. This book outlines the lessons I've found critical on that journey – so far.

Oh, and I've also still never worked for a Fortune 500 company, but there's time yet.

UPWARDS

ONE: SAY GOOD MORNING

I stumbled into case management with the grace of a newly born giraffe. I was stationed at a hospital in Norfolk by a skilled nursing facility (SNF) organization and given the direction to "convince clients to choose our SNF and get as many orthopedic patients as possible." (For those in the healthcare field, this was before total joint replacements were removed from the inpatient only list. For everyone who doesn't know: orthopedic patients yield high revenues for SNFs.)

I was 24 years old, had no sales experience, and very little training on how to fulfil my mission. But I gamely showed up at that hospital every day and tried to speak to patients who needed rehabilitation services when they were ready for discharge. While I was tilting at that particular windmill and making none of my quotas, I discovered case management.

I had seen case management as a floor nurse but didn't really understand who they were or what they did. In my doomed-from-the-beginning sales job, I got to see what they did from a different perspective. I hung outside their office and eavesdropped as much as possible, because I found their work fascinating.

About six months into that sales job, the healthcare system that owned the hospital underwent a significant reorganization. They centralized their utilization review function, meaning the case managers at the hospital would focus on discharge planning and length of stay management and the central team would focus on authorizations. I don't know the behind-the-scenes politics or how this change was communicated, but I saw one person after the other resign from the case management department.

Seeing an opportunity to abandon my ill-fated sales job and become a case manager, I printed out my resume and walked to Sherry's office. Sherry was the manager of the department, and I hadn't interacted with her at all. I had no idea if my boldness would be rewarded or not, but I figured it was worth a shot.

As I stood in her open doorway, she half turned to me with an extremely annoyed expression. She finished her phone conversation, hung up, and asked me what I wanted – not impolitely, but I could tell she wasn't having her best day. When I held out my resume and said I was interested in joining her team, she gave a short laugh.

"That was the third resignation this week. How many jobs do you want?"

I just wanted one, which she was gracious enough to offer me. And so, I became a case manager.

Sherry was a godsend to me. She was my first mentor, and I will always hold a special place in my heart for her. After a year of being the emergency department case manager and weekend utilization review nurse (the centralized department didn't do ED screenings for admission status), I was promoted to supervisor. This is where the newborn giraffe analogy really comes into focus.

I had no idea how to be a supervisor, but I wanted desperately to be in leadership. By that point in my career, I knew I was going into leadership and administration, but I didn't have a clear picture as to how. Sherry saw something in me – a very new case manager who was probably annoyingly ambitious – and decided to pour into me.

My promotion came at the same time the hospital opened its new wing. Part of the new construction was office space for my department. This meant I had my own office, right across the hall from Sherry, and a shared office about ten feet down the hall where the rest of the team congregated to document and decompress. I loved this set up, and the feeling of accomplishment of having my own office was intense.

My typical morning routine was to come in the back door, near the shared workspace, walk to my office, and start working. This seemed like a very efficient routine. I didn't drink coffee from the shared coffee maker by the sink alcove in the hallway. I didn't stop and chit-chat about my weekend or what show I was watching on TV (this was before Netflix, so people also talked about commercials they had seen, which I found bizarre. I have never willingly watched a commercial – with one specific exception.)

My routine was the peak of professionalism and discipline. I was focused. I was a machine!

And Sherry found that very problematic.

It was perhaps a few months into this new position, and our new space, when Sherry came to my office and closed the door behind her. That was never a good sign.

She eased into the conversation by asking me how I thought it was going with the team. How was my transition to supervisor? I couldn't wait to tell her how awesome it all was, and how much work I was doing, and how great the team was.

"The team doesn't feel you support them."

My brain ground to a halt so quickly I think I actually heard the screeching of rubber on pavement.

"What do you mean the team doesn't feel I support them?"

"You come in every morning and go straight to your office and work."

"Yeah."

She waited a beat; I think in hope that I would have a sudden epiphany and understand what she was talking about.

After mentally gathering herself, and maybe internally debating if the precocious idiot in front of her was worth her trouble, she said, "you never say good morning."

I don't think I had ever said good morning to anyone in my life. Morning greetings weren't really a thing in my household growing up. I'm sure my mom said good morning before school, and I am sure I grunted at her and poured myself some coffee. I have no recollection of if my sister and I ever said good morning to each other – I think she woke up and immediately launched into full conversations or something. My dad has definitely never said "good morning" outside of conversations he has had in his fake-but-professional phone voice.

I did not understand a single word coming out of Sherry's mouth. I had suddenly been transported to bizarro land where meaningless ritualistic greetings were more important than doing 10 hours of work in an 8-hour day.

Sensing my mental gears were still grinding, Sherry broke it down further.

"You have to make them feel like you care about them, even if you don't."

"I do care about them. What does that have to do with saying good morning?"

"Think about it. If I just walked by you and never greeted you, wouldn't you feel I don't care about you as a person?"

"No. I would assume you had work to do."

"Okay robot, well the humans like it when you say good morning, so you have to start doing that effectively immediately."

She didn't actually say that last line, but that was definitely what she meant, and it was what I heard. She didn't explicitly threaten to disown or fire me if I didn't start saying good morning, but it was heavily implied that the repercussions of my failing to follow this order would be swift and unpleasant.

The next day I walked into the office, marched to the open doorway of the shared space, and looked at the group gathered there. They were going through their morning ritual of drinking coffee, printing out the patient assignments for the day, and talking about personal stuff. (Back then, "personal stuff" is how I characterized any conversation that wasn't about work.)

They all turned to look at me, stuck in the doorway like a frozen specter of missed good mornings.

In the stiffest and most unnatural way a human being could ever speak, I said "good morning," turned and marched to my office. It was my finest work in social ineptitude.

Sherry, who had heard the entire exchange from her office, turned in her chain and stared at me through both our open doorways in what I can only describe as annoyed incomprehension. Her facial expression was the living embodied of "really?!?"

"I said good morning," I said, still in robot mode.

"Yes," she drawled, elongating the 's' for effect. "Now, do it every day."

"Fine."

And then I turned back to my computer and did some *real* work, having already wasted at least 5 minutes of my precious time.

Here is what the young and immature version of me did not understand – you can do a lot for people, but if you don't connect to them as human beings, all your work will be for naught. Maya Angelou, a source of profound wisdom in this world, said it best when she said, "I've learned that people will forget what you said, people will forget what you did, but people will never forget how you made them feel."

This is critical leadership lesson number one. It wasn't about saying good morning or not – it was about how I made my team feel. People want to feel a connection to their work, their boss, and their origination. Without that connection, we don't feel as though our work, or we as people, matter. And everyone wants to matter.

Understanding that people want to feel as though they matter may be one of the foundational building blocks of emotional intelligence. Mental Health American defines emotional intelligence, in part, as the ability to understand the emotions of people around you. If we understand that people will be impacted by our words and action, we can adjust our behavior accordingly, and start to build relationships.

The relationship between emotional intelligence, connection, and relationships can be drawn like this:

My clumsy greeting that morning was the beginning of a profound personal journey. It would take me a few years, but I would come to understand that all my work was meaningless if people did not like working with me. I genuinely wanted to serve my team, but serving doesn't mean completing tasks or doing work no one else wants to do. Serving means putting other people first – not putting their work first, or their technical needs, but putting them first as people.

The first stop on the road to building genuine relationships might be as simple as a morning greeting. Sherry taught me, among other things, to always say "good morning."

TWO: IT'S ALL ABOUT RELATIONSHIPS

The oft-cited corporate tagline "it's all about relationships" has been so overplayed that it's almost trite. Because we've heard our parents preach it, and read incalculable leadership articles on LinkedIn, that all espouse the importance of relationships and networking, we've become numb to it. The advice about relationships is almost white noise. Or worse yet, we ascribe the ability to network as something reserved for the wealthy and connected-by-birth.

My first mentor, Sherry, tried to impart upon me the importance of building relationships. She is a natural networker and gifted at nurturing new connections. Those skills are not inherent to my personality; I have to work at it. Despite hearing from my mentor that this skill was critical, I made mostly half-hearted attempts to master it. It wasn't until about a decade into my leadership journey that I realized just how critical building relationships is.

Networking gets a smarmy reputation, because we tend to think of it as a mechanism to get something, or to promote our careers. For the conniving among us, I'm sure that description of networking is accurate. At its core, though, networking is simply building relationships with people. That sounds simple, but it's actually challenging for those who don't have that natural skill.

A book that had a profound impact on me was *Quiet: The Power of Introverts in a World That Can't Stop Talking*, by Susan Cain. Before reading Quiet, I was adept at rationalizing my lack of networking to myself. I told myself my work would be judged by itself, and if it was good enough people would reach out to me. That meritocracy-based business model was a flop. I had somehow forgotten that people aren't telepathic – my work wouldn't be magically transmitted into their brains.

Without networking, my opportunities to share my work were limited.

I made fits and starts in the building-relationships arena during the first few years of my leadership journey. If someone approached me and wanted to connect, I would do so, but I didn't know how to cultivate those relationships. I didn't know how to be the one to reach out.

I met John through a company my healthcare system contracted with. John was a physician who, late in his career, was focusing on utilization review and physician advisor services. He was brash, outspoken, and he liked talking to me. At the time I met John I hadn't fully internalized the importance of relationships. I had it in my head that the company I was working for at that time was my forever home. I had fantasies of retiring there after 40 years with a great pension (I was one of the last generations of hires to have a pension at that organization) and an even better reputation. Since I was never going to leave that healthcare system, I figured my world didn't have to expand much.

It could have also been that I wasn't thinking big enough yet. My world hadn't expanded, and I was under the false belief I understood what my career path would look like. Compounding this small-mindedness was the fact that I was in recovery from a violent marriage and still in the early phases of trauma therapy. I have to look back on my younger and more guarded self with empathy, because otherwise I tend to judge her rather harshly.

Younger me was very smart – at least about processes and facts and figures. Not so much about people. Younger me knew things John didn't know. I could quote certain regulations and hospital billing facts that he couldn't. I also had thick walls around my emotional self and used my intellect as a defense mechanism. That looks like un-checked ego, for those who haven't had the pleasure of working with someone like my younger self.

When John was laid off from his company and founded his own consulting company, it at first seemed like I would come along for the ride. I thought I could help with writing copy or doing speaking engagements.

But I left all the heavy lifting of that relationship to John –
I didn't meet him in the middle.

Meeting someone in the middle means being the
first to reach out. It means being gracious. Most
importantly, it means humility. Younger me was a much
more exasperated and less patient person than I am now,
and it showed in how I treated that relationship.

For me, humility means valuing the contributions
of all people, regardless of what those contributions are. It
means valuing what people can teach me. It means valuing
everyone as a person; meaning I acknowledge the inherent
value a person has simply because they are a human being
that deserves that acknowledgement.

Younger me was a little bit of a dolt, though, so I
didn't do any of that. Instead, I acted like an advisor to
John; someone who was available should their lauded
expertise be needed. John was in his sixties or seventies
and had a distinguished career – he did not need an
advisor. In that moment, having lost his job and starting
his own venture, he probably needed a friend. And I could

have fulfilled that role. I'd like to think the current version of me would be that friend.

Humans are social creatures. Even the most introverted among us need connection. The prefrontal cortex and temporoparietal junction parts of our brains are wired for connection. There's an amazing book written on this subject by Dr. Matt Lieberman. In his book *Social: Why Our Brains Are Wired to Connect*, he explains the neural networks responsible for social thinking and connection. As a psychiatric mental health nurse practitioner, I find the science of human connections fascinating.

Social connections activate the pleasure centers of our brains. From an evolutionary standpoint, this makes complete sense. At the dawn of humanity, humans had to work together for their very survival. Our species depended on humans getting along – on connecting. In 2023, the U.S. Surgeon General's office published an 82-page exposé on what they called "the epidemic of loneliness." They stated in that publication that loneliness and social isolation increase the risk of premature death by 26% - 29%, and that a lack of social connection increases risk by the same percentage as smoking fifteen cigarettes a day. Basically, lack of connection kills us about as fast as a pack-a-day habit.

Networking is not about career climbing, though it certainly is critical to professional growth; it's about building relationships to improve our wellness and the wellness of others. We need each other. We need each other for encouragement, reproach, education, and general wellbeing.

When scrolling through the endless LinkedIn feed of influencers and attending conferences where we don't know anyone, it's helpful to remember that everyone is a person. Everyone is seeking connection. Everyone wants relationships. Let's remember our visual of emotional intelligence, human connection, and relationships:

Somewhere in the crowd is a person who will give us encouragement or speak words of wisdom and affirmation into our lives. Someone might even give us the big break we've been waiting for. If we venture into crowded waters seeking connection, we will find one. If we view every relationship as an opportunity to connect genuinely and authentically, we will build the strongest foundation of growth conceivable – both professionally and personally.

My mindset now when I walk into a crowded room, even though I still have that tiny pang of social anxiety that makes me want to find a quiet corner, is that of connection and openness. To build genuine connections, we must have radical openness, the concept of which deserves its own chapter.

Before we move on to radical openness – a final word about John. When I left the organization I thought I would retire from, the emotional toll was heavy. I grieved that job change for a long time. In leaving that company, I also left a lot of relationships, including those that were just burgeoning. Younger me didn't understand the power of connections, and so I didn't nurture the relationships I had already built. Like leaves on the vine, relationships will wither if the root of them isn't tended. I lost many connections, and people who could have been my friends and mentors, because I didn't think to water our vines.

THREE: YOU NEED RADICAL OPENNESS

I don't think you can build connections without radical openness. There are a few other things you can't do either, but we'll get to that. First, a little more about connections and how they relate to openness.

2020 was not a great year for me. I'm sure no one reading this can relate to that.

My team suddenly pivoted to remote, growth opportunities dried up, promotions and hiring ground to a halt, and survival, rather than innovation, became the goal. That happened to be the year that I had my first speaking engagements scheduled. I had developed a relationship with an executive at an organization that had a very long reach. Think: one of the largest healthcare related organizations in the country. I was tripping over myself to work with them.

He had asked me if I was interested in speaking at numerous conferences and meetings his organization hosted. I had been thinking about consulting for a while at that point but thought I would do it part-time while maintaining a position at my happily-ever-after-company. Striking out on my own, in my own business, was not a fully formed thought at that time (though little embers of a dream were always ready to be stoked).

When COVID shut down the world, all my engagements were either cancelled or changed to virtual. This was when we all were still scrambling to figure out how to work and learn remotely, and virtual conferences weren't common (at least in my field). Suddenly, my amazing plans of being flown across the country to speak in the Bay Area, Texas, and Baltimore were dashed. There were no speaking engagements coming my way that year. I think I spoke at one virtual conference, but that was it.

I was left at loose ends. My team was mature enough that they didn't need much from me on a day-to-day basis. The system level work I was accustomed to, mainly process improvement and project management, had evaporated overnight. There quite literally was not enough work for me to do. This led to a few dominoes falling in my career, and the short version is I left my forever-company. We'll talk more about that in the next chapter.

Fast forward a few years, and I was asked to speak at a conference again. I had been an ostrich for about three years at that point. The blog I had cultivated before COVID was dusty and long silent. I had facilitated workshops and brainstorming sessions as part of my new roles, but I hadn't given speeches to large crowds. By this point, I had switched jobs a couple of times, and I was just trying to figure out what my career was going to look like. I was also finishing my doctorate degree nurse practitioner certification (at the same time, which I don't recommend) and was still workshopping what to do with my degrees when I graduated. I knew I was supposed to pursue my nurse practitioner qualifications, but beyond that my path had yet to be illuminated.

I'm not sure why Autumn even thought to ask me to speak at the conference she was helping to organize, other than we had met in person at an annual leadership meeting and she liked me. (The importance of connections!)

I was dusty and crusty, as my Gen Z children would say, when I showed up in West Virginia to speak to a crowd for the first time in three years. I didn't know a single person at this conference, other than Autumn, and she was so sick she couldn't speak – so using her as a social shield for the entire two days was not a viable plan. On my way to West Virginia, being it's a long drive, I did what I normally do on solo road trips and called my sister.

Melinda is a natural connection builder. She's the extrovert to my introvert. I used to call her a social butterfly when we were kids. She's also the most spiritually aware human I have ever met. I am blessed to have a sister that speaks God's words into my life, and I hope I do the same for her sometimes. I don't recall the entirety of our conversation, but I know we talked about divine intervention and what we were both supposed to be doing with our lives.

Something in that conversation inspired me to walk into that hotel conference room with what I call radical openness. Radical openness, to me, is the willingness to receive. In this case, it was the willingness to receive social connections. At other times in my career, radical openness has looked like the willingness to change my mind or be taught something new. I find that form of radical openness comes more easily than the social form.

In the setting of this conference, radical openness looked like open body language and a friendly expression. I'm very conscious of what my face and body are doing in social settings, which is not something everyone has to deliberately focus on. I have to make conscious decisions about these things, though. If I'm not mindful of my nonverbal communication, I will come across as closed off. So, I opened my body language.

I sat at a table of people I didn't know and tried to make small talk – I had limited success. I was invited to dinner with people I had never met and had much more success at being part of the conversation. I made some amazing connections in that one dinner that I plan to nurture forever. I also made sure that after I finished my presentation, I was open to meeting everyone in that room. If they had feedback for me, I wanted to hear it. If they wanted to talk about the topic I'd spoken on, I gladly shared more. If they wanted me to ride a mechanical bull… I drew a line in the sand, there. There really is only so much extroverting I can do before I shrivel inside. I adamantly refused to get on the mechanical bull.

At this conference, I met Susan. Susan might be the nicest person I have ever had the fortune of meeting. Not only is she genuinely nice, but she is also an excellent relationship builder. Susan was the person who suggested I speak at a conference in North Carolina and then also gave my name to the planning board of that conference. At that North Carolina conference, I met people who connected me to other people – and suddenly opportunities for speaking engagements were everywhere.

I haven't mentioned it yet, but I love speaking engagements. I am an introvert who loves getting on stage and speaking on topics I'm passionate about, though I do need some recharging time after. My deepest desire, for a long time, was to break into what I called the 'lecture circuit.' I didn't know how to do that, though, and so I put that dream in a box and put the box on a darkened shelf in my heart. A few years after shelving that dream, the how was revealed to me – I would turn that dream into a reality through connections. I would build those connections through radical openness.

It's important for me to note that radical openness, whatever form it takes, cannot be faked. I cannot fake being interested in people. I cannot fake wanting to hear their stories. I cannot fake being kind. I am going to be genuine in being those things, or I cannot be them at all. The fake-it-till-you-make-it mentality can work for things, but it does not work for building connections and relationships.

The reason radical openness resonates so much with me, is because it is fundamentally built upon humility. Without humility, there can be no openness to learn. There can be no openness to the concept we may be wrong. If we don't have those beliefs, how can there be room for newness? How can there be room to be mentored?

In my younger leadership years, humility was my most significant area of opportunity. That's corporate speak for 'weakness.'

It's not that I thought very highly of myself; in fact, my self-esteem was in the toilet for much of my early career. The lack of humility was related to a few things: being young, being smart, and needing defense mechanisms a mile high and ten miles deep. I used a lack of humility as a wall to keep others at a safe distance. Through a lot of work and soul-searching, I broke those walls down. Only then could I truly learn how to be humble.

Humility doesn't look like false modesty or being self-deprecating. Though I am self-deprecating, and I think it's mostly hilarious. To me, humility looks like radical openness. Humility is the belief in the possibility of being wrong, in learning new things, in meeting amazing people, and valuing experiences for the simple reason that all experiences are opportunities to grow.

If I were going to map the relationship between these concepts, it would look something like this:

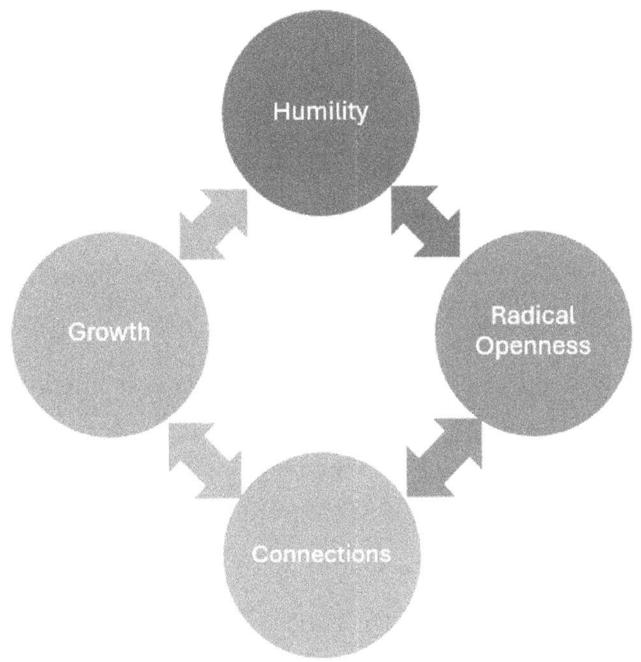

In his book *The Ideal Team Player*, Patrick Lencioni defines humility as lacking excessive ego and being quick to point out the contributions of others. From a psychological perspective, humility is the understanding that we are no better or worse than anyone else. Basically, we have all equal status and worth as human beings. Our talents and gifts may be different, but they are equal in weight. I think of humility as an antidote to shame – we are all people living lives and we all have equal value, regardless of any of our inherited or earned circumstances, or lack thereof.

The Association for Behavioral and Cognitive Therapies (ABCT) defines radical openness as a willingness to doubt or question ourselves without falling apart. ABCT states that facts can be misleading because we don't know what we don't know. They're referencing our internal facts, or beliefs, which could be things like "I know what I'm doing," or "I'm an expert in this thing."

Radical openness is a significant aspect of a particular type of therapy, aptly named radical openness dialectical behavior therapy (RO-DBT). Interestingly, this therapy is specifically designed to treat 'overcontrol.' Overcontrolled people are those who see unfamiliar situations as dangerous, or intimidating, rather than exciting and rewarding. Overcontrolled individuals hide their emotions and make it challenging for others to get to know their true selves.

RO-DBT targets loneliness and isolation by helping clients build social connection skills. Part of building those skills using this therapeutic modality is helping clients build neural pathways between the social and safety parts of the brain by engaging in deliberate body postures, facial expression, genuine self-disclosure, and playfulness.

It's fascinating that a therapeutic technique specifically designed to increase openness focuses on social connections – bolstering my belief that these two things are intrinsically related. Isn't it also interesting that one of the skills RO-DBT teaches is how to open body language, exhibit a warm and open expression, and genuinely self-disclose? If we're aware of what our face is doing, we can adjust it appropriately, and exhibit openness. Showing openness is just as important as internally experiencing it, so ensuring we're aligning our internal landscape with our external expression is important.

Having the belief that we don't know what we don't know and we're open to learning is the basis of humility, which is needed for radical openness. Radical openness is needed to build connections. Radical openness is also needed to maintain humility – it's a bidirectional flow, which is why the arrows in the model go both ways. Openness will yield connections, and more connections will encourage us to continue being open – again a bidirectional relationship!

Defining what radical openness looks like for you will help you understand if you need to work on developing humility. Radical openness may not look like the need to increase social connections – that may be your strength. Perhaps radical openness looks like the openness to new ideas. Perhaps it looks like openness to changing process. Perhaps it looks like innovation in your industry. It may even look like increasing your tolerance of risk taking. Whatever you define as your greatest area of opportunity, embodying radical openness in your everyday life is guaranteed to lead to growth.

Even if you're a gifted relationship builder, radical openness will help you build more, and deeper, connections. If you're radically open, humble, and building connections, you are primed and ready for growth.

FOUR: BE READY

Speaking of ready!

We need to be ready. As a young leader, I was nominated to participate in a leadership development program. The program was designed for up-and-coming leaders, provided information, and taught skills leaders need to be successful. I am so grateful my leaders saw something in me and nominated me for that program. That experience was the foundation I built future leadership development programs on, and I now design and facilitate similar programs to the ones I benefited from.

During that experience, I met the facilitator of the company's leadership development program, Tonya. Tonya was a dynamic speaker, and she had an obvious passion for leadership development. She was the facilitator for all three of the programs I went through at that organization.

After successful completion of each program, there was a commencement ceremony. All the participants, and their bosses, would gather in a hotel conference room, and completion certificates would be presented. As part of the ceremony, a student from each cohort was selected to give a graduation speech, much like the valedictorian of a high school. Tonya would select someone she believed would speak on behalf of the entire cohort to share their experience, what they learned, and why the program was beneficial.

I was well familiar with this routine by the time I completed the third and final leadership development course. This was before I understood networking, but I enjoyed getting to go to the ceremony and see everyone who had completed the different courses that semester.

About a week before the ceremony, Tonya called me.

She shared that the person who was scheduled to speak on behalf of my cohort was unable to do so and she wondered if I would do it. Any answer other than 'yes' did not even occur to me. It was an honor for her to ask me, never mind that I was second choice. (I may have been the third choice and someone else turned her down. I don't know, and I choose to believe I was a remarkably close second choice.)

I spent a lot of time on that speech. It was perhaps five minutes long, so nothing like the keynotes I give now, but it was my first time speaking on a stage. That little ember of desire in me, the one shaped like public speaking and consulting and entrepreneurialism, turned into a small flame. I wanted to do a good job so badly it made my teeth ache.

I like to think that these days I can speak to anyone, anywhere, anytime. I have practiced my social skills and public speaking, and people tell me I never look nervous on stage. I am living proof that these skills can be learned – because I did not have them when Tonya asked me to get on that stage.

The moments leading up to my speech were like a time warp. Minutes passed by like a snail stuck in molasses in January, yet they were also flying by faster than I could keep up with. I have no idea what anyone said in the speeches that came before me. After what felt like no time at all and at least a year, Tonya stood up to introduce me.

She stood behind the lectern and shared that the person who was initially scheduled to speak couldn't make it.

"So, I asked myself who could do it with such short notice. Who could be ready like that? And there was one person in this cohort who is the embodiment of 'be ready.' So, welcome to the stage Tabitha Hapeman."

My hands were shaking so badly I could barely hold my notes. My voice was shaking even worse, and I'm fairly sure it cracked at least once. It was not a brilliant speech – I'm not even sure it was a good one. But it was mine, and it was my first, and I treasured being on that stage.

It wasn't until I got home, and after the adrenaline dump that accompanied my new accomplishment, that I reflected on what Tonya said. She had perceived me as the embodiment of the concept 'be ready.' I had never envisioned myself in that way.

Up until that point in my career, I had a few jobs. I jumped from wanting to be a psychiatric nurse before graduation, to starting my career in medical-surgical nursing, to pediatric home care, to occupational travel nursing (just one gig, though), to sales, and then to case management. In hindsight, I was always ready to try something new and I wasn't overly concerned about failing. At the time, though, I just thought I was good at taking opportunities when they came along. I didn't think about the concept of always being ready.

When we think about readiness in leadership, typically we're thinking about what the development industry calls "the readiness gap." This is the gap that exists between people that are ready to step into leadership roles, and the actual need that exists for good leaders. It's also about the gap between knowledge and action.

In the 2023 Deloitte *Global Human Capital Trends* report, researchers found that 50% of all organizations' leaders were struggling to identify their priorities. 94% of respondents said leadership capabilities and effectiveness were critical to the organization's success, but only 23% said their leaders had the capabilities necessary to reach those goals. The gap between 94% and 23% is pretty wide.

Leadership today, I would argue, is more challenging than ever before. Some of that is because we're more aware of previous societal failings and are learning to adapt and overcome them. I firmly believe in diversity and inclusion, but I also recognize that these initiatives are coming while people are still learning how to lead a diverse team, meaning they're building the plane while they're flying it. Now more than ever, teams can diversify, as so much of the global workforce can work from anywhere. That is both a huge opportunity, and a potential for conflict.

Overcoming the ills of the past and gaining the skills to lead a diverse team are a small part of the puzzle, though. Leaders today must do a lot. They need to know a lot. They are mastering multiple software systems, they need to be technical experts, they should have the communication skills of a therapist, and the forethought of an industry visionary. That is a tall order.

Especially in the past few years, businesses have grown extremely ambitious. It's not that capitalism hasn't always pushed businesses to grow and compete – that's always been true. Now, though, the rate of change and innovation is exponentially faster than in previous decades. As businesses change and expand, so too must their leaders – leaving an already under-pressure group grasping to keep up.

Compounding this is the industry research that tells us we won't have enough qualified and prepared leaders to replace those on the cusp of retirement. With all this doom and gloom, how can leaders hope to be ready? And what are they trying to be ready for?

I've pondered this and I think readiness is the openness to new experiences and willingness to learn. Perhaps it's also the willingness to try, which I think is closely related. If willingness is a key component of readiness, so too is preparation.

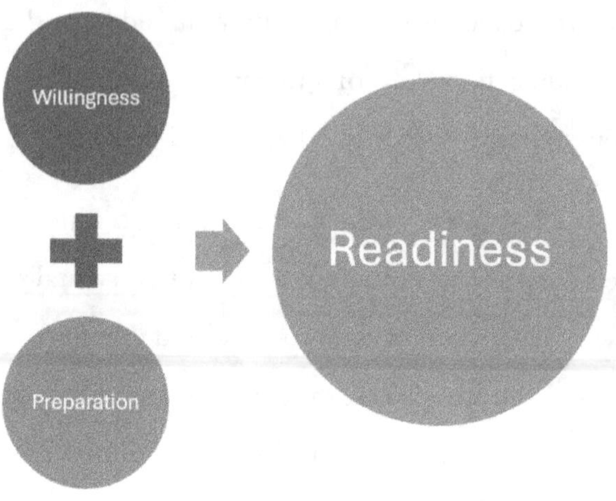

Preparation does not mean understanding every nuance of a particular task or change. I have worked with leaders who get what my friend and coworker Lisa calls "analysis paralysis." This is where the need to understand every nuance and minuscule detail stops leaders from making decisions and taking actions. I relate this closely to "death by committee," which is just as painful to experience and as likely to result in meaningless conversation and no action.

My mental image of leaders desperate to have all the facts before they are prepared to make a decision is that of someone in quicksand. I grew up in the 90s, and I was given to believe that quicksand would be a much more significant part of my life than it has been. I have never actually encountered it, but I have vivid mental pictures. Quicksand and the Bermuda Triangle were prevalent in my thought processes during my childhood, but I haven't heard anything about either of them recently. Either someone solved both those problems or they were over advertised when I was growing up. But I digress.

The leader is stuck in quicksand. They are frozen and cannot move and believe that just one more piece of information will be the branch they need to pull themselves free. Worse yet, some leaders are happily stuck in their slowly sinking gritty ooze and are just pulling pieces of information towards them, putting them like rocks in their pockets as they get sucked deeper into the mire.

Preparation is not expertise. Preparation is laying the groundwork. Merriam-Webster defines preparation as: *"the action or process of making something ready for use or service or of getting ready for some occasion, test, or duty."*

Leaders prepare in a lot of different ways, but a big aspect of being prepared as a leader is being flexible.

Understanding what flexibility isn't, can help us further understand what it is. The opposite of flexibility is rigidity. From a mental health perspective, rigidity is the source of significant suffering.

Rigidity is the inability to adapt to new information. Rigid thinking is the desire for predictability and a compulsion to complete certain actions. Rigid leaders refuse to take in new information, either passively or actively. They continue doing what they've always done because that's what they're comfortable with. They hate when plans change, or may actively resist changing, even in the face of irrefutable evidence that change is necessary. Rigid leaders are the 'my way or the highway' managers that stifle creatively and chase eager and ambitious employees away. Now that we've clearly outlined rigidity, it's easier to define flexibility.

We teach psychological flexibility in mental health. One of the first modalities I was exposed to in my career was ACT – Acceptance and Commitment Therapy. I had a rudimentary understanding of cognitive behavioral therapy (CBT) from my schooling, but ACT was the first discipline I dove into and studied. When I worked in development for a mental health care company, I got to spend a significant amount of time on the units and with the clients. I loved this, and I also loved helping the teams I worked with build therapeutic services and processes, but I was a novice in therapeutic modalities (that's a fancy term for types of therapies).

To help me gain a deeper understanding of the therapy clients were receiving, my boss at the time introduced me to ACT. Chad was an ACT practitioner and he introduced me to the concept of psychological flexibility as a curative for suffering. His philosophy was that thoughts and emotions were fleeting and unreliable sources of decision making. He taught me that psychological flexibility allows people to balance competing desires and needs, redirect their internal resources as needed, and live life free of the pain from traumatic memories and experiences. A layperson's guide to ACT would include mindfulness, acknowledging feelings and thoughts without ruminating in them, and living according to values.

When I think of both willingness and preparation, I think of ACT. Are we willing to experience new things?

Willing or not, we will never escape newness and novelty; we cannot prevent change. Are we willing to learn and experiment and fail? Are we prepared to pivot? Are we constantly learning new skills and information? If we maintain both willingness and preparedness as core skills, then we will be always we ready.

Ready for what – we don't and can't know. Ready for opportunity, perhaps. Ready for the next amazing thing that is coming down the pike. Most importantly, perhaps, is ready to be the best version of ourselves.

FIVE: PRESSURE IS A PRIVILEGE

When I left my forever-but-not-really company, I made a career pivot. I decided I had gone as far as I could go in the niche field I had been in for a decade. This was a very short-sighted thought, and I re-pivoted a couple of years later, but I'm grateful for that harsh determination now. I got a job as what I like to call a 'fixer.' My title had the term 'development' in it, but I was really deployed in different settings to figure out how to improve the client experience and the services we were delivering.

When I took the job, I was told we were opening a 100-bed substance use disorder facility. That sounded like an amazing mission, and I was excited to be a part of it.

There was some critical information I was lacking until I officially came on board, though.

I was sitting in the little conference room, which was just large enough to hold a massive mahogany table and six office chairs. We only had 4 chairs, though, because there were only 4 of us in the room. Chad had gathered his intrepid team to talk through the plan to open the facility. In the room were me, Chad, Jonathon, and Mike. I had been there about a week, mostly focused on completing the computer-based training programs assigned to all new hires, Mike had just started, and Jonathon had been on board about a year.

It was in this meeting I began to understand what was actually happening. Jonathon had quite literally been a solo employee trying to prepare to open this facility while COVID had halted all progress, including construction. He had written all the policies needed for the state board, but actual direct planning had been nonexistent.

"We've got to get opened." Chad was obviously under a lot of pressure.

"Okay, when are opening?" I thought this was a very reasonable question.

Chad looked at me and I swear I felt the gravity of his gaze pushing me into the floor. "30 days."

And so began the wildest professional ride I have ever been on (thus far).

"Okay, who have we hired?"

"You three."

"How are we going to hire enough people to open in 30 days?"

"We'll have a hiring event. Mass hiring."

"Where are the training materials for people we're going to hire?"

"That's your job, Hapeman. Write them."

I am now dissociating and floating away from my body. "Where are the policies and procedures and SOPs we need to function?" I ask, like a calm and reasonable professional.

"Hapeman, you seem to be confused. That's your job. Write them."

I can hear the harps playing at my funeral. They beckon me with their calming resonance. I ask the final question I can bear to ask. "Who's going to train all these new hires?"

"Hapeman…" Chad is now staring at me as though I have asked him to explain to me where babies come from. "You are."

And then I perished, the end.

No, not really. Because Tonya said I was the embodiment of readiness. So, it was time to be ready. Not get ready, because there was no time for that, I needed to jump straight into being ready.

Let me be clear: I was not an expert in opening new substance use disorder facilities. I had never participated in de novo growth before. The experience I had around new facilities was that of mergers and acquisitions. I understood that process, and the onboarding of new sites, but a new start up was something outside my wheelhouse. My entire life became consumed with research. I pulled every article, every publicly available bit of information, every peer reviewed journal available to me through my graduate school library. I consumed them all voraciously in an effort to open this facility without looking like a complete idiot.

Along the way I became a certified de-escalation trainer. Not certified in de-escalation. No, I skipped that part and went right to becoming a trainer. And I trained about 100 people in de-escalation the first few months I was with this company. Be ready, indeed.

We did not open in 30 days, it was 60 (and we opened only a few beds at first), but the monumental effort that went into that endeavor was something I will forever be proud of. When we opened, I thought the hardest part was over. People had been hired. People were trained – mostly, it was still a work in progress. Clients were starting to be served and a need in the community was being met. It was time to pump the brakes.

And then came Chad.

I love Chad, and I joined that organization because of him. He is a phenomenal leader, and I learned more from him in 2 years than I thought was possible. But he was also a harbinger of news, which I wouldn't classify as 'bad,' but it tended to be less than good.

Chad sat in my office, perhaps for the first time ever. Normally we were in the conference room, which had become the 'war room.' "We're scheduled for our Joint Commission survey."

"Okay, great."

Chad is now looking at me expectedly, as though he is waiting for me to say something more intelligent. He must be disappointed, because I don't have anything further to offer in regard to the information he had just provided to me.

"Are you ready?" he asks me.

Somehow, when I was around Chad, I doubted every single instance in my life when someone told me I was intelligent. He had this amazing ability to stump me entirely.

"Ready for what?"

"For the accreditation survey."

"Sure, I mean, I can speak to the training and the onboarding process."

Chad's disappointment with this comment seemed immeasurable. He decided to spell this out for me like I am a child, which seems appropriate for this encounter. "Hapeman, you're going to lead the survey."

I recalled talking about this during my initial interview, but the past 60 days had so completely fried my internal hard drive that I required further explanation. "You mean someone from corporate will be here and I'll be the on-site point person, right?"

Leaning forward, with his elbows resting on his knees, Chad made intense eye contact with me. "Hapeman, you're leading the accreditation survey. You have joint commission experience."

Here is a fun story about my interview process for this job: when Chad asked me if I had accreditation experience, I answered in the affirmative. I was the lead person for utilization review for all hospitals in my system when DNV came for our surveys. The key term there is 'DNV,' which is a different accreditation agency than Joint

Commission. Also critical are the facts that I was responsible for a single department, in which I was an expert, and all my experience was in acute care.

The only experience I had with Joint Commission was when I was a floor nurse, and the nurse manager would careen up and down the halls telling us to hide our drinks. I was a night nurse, and my interaction with survey teams was limited, because they all happened during the day. All I knew was to keep my coffee hidden in the drawer under the desk, so no one saw it that week. (When that week was over, the coffee was back on the desk).

I had no experience with accreditation outside of a hospital. I certainly had no experience with substance use disorder facilities. During the interview process, I failed to clarify that my experience with accreditation did not extend to Joint Commission.

But I am ready. So, down the rabbit hole I went. I printed the accreditation standards, which took a lot of paper, and I read every line. I must have looked a bit possessed, sitting in my office pouring over hundreds of pages with a highlighter and little sticky 'sign here' notes that marked areas I needed to focus on.

If opening a facility in 60 days was a lot of pressure, leading the entire accreditation survey process while being watched by every member of the corporate C-suite was like being compressed in a vice. The accreditor was on Zoom, as was I and about twenty other people, most of whom were in the top leadership positions in the company. If I wasn't successful in getting us accredited, the failure would be extremely public.

I don't want to paint the picture that I was the only person speaking while this VIP audience looked on. There were great people that helped me, and service line leaders spoke to their areas. Thank God the system director of nursing spoke to her processes and the system director of compliance spoke to her area. They were instrumental in our success, but the majority of the process was squarely bound up and placed on my shoulders.

I love sports documentaries. I watch every single one on every streaming service I have a subscription to. I was watching a tennis documentary, and as the camera panned out across the player entrance to Arthur Ashe Stadium, I saw a plaque in the background. I paused the show to re-read it because it seemed so profound.

"Pressure is a Privilege" - Billie Jean King.

I am not a fan of watching sports, with few exceptions. I love sports documentaries because the psychology of sports, sport leadership, and human endurance is fascinating to me. I focus on those aspects, not the actual sport being played. This means I can watch hours and hours of these documentaries and have a very rudimentary understanding of the sport itself. All that is to say that I hadn't heard of Billie Jean King before I saw that plaque and googled her name.

Billie Jean King has won thirty-nine grand slams, founded the Women's Tennis Association and the Women's Sport Foundation, and might be the greatest tennis player of all time. King wrote a book called *Pressure is a Privilege*, which is what the title of this chapter borrows from. King explains that if there is no pressure, then there are no expectations. The only people who don't feel pressure are those of whom nothing is expected.

She equates pressure to opportunity, in that most of the time when we feel under pressure it's because something incredible is before us. Without pressure, we can never know what we're capable of. If we don't come up to serve in the last round of Wimbledon, will we ever know how truly great we are?

I believe there is greatness in all of us. The only difference between showcasing that greatness and not is the willingness to endure pressure and expecting yourself to rise to meet it. That's an important equation, and it looks like this:

Greatness is not a set of inherited or inherent characteristics. There are no special people destined for greatness – only those willing to endure the pressure and rise to meet the challenge. One of my favorite books, *Grit,*

by Angela Duckworth, examined why some people are successful in their endeavors and some are not. She tested the common theory that success is dependent on talent and found that, somewhat counterintuitively, those with the greatest natural talent were more likely to fail. That's because those with more natural talent tended to be praised for the ease with which they did things. Those with less natural talent had to work harder to be successful.

She found that no matter the amount of natural talent, those willing to endure – those with grit – were the most successful. This isn't to say that people with natural talents or abilities are destined to fail, but if those people rely only on their God given gifts and don't put the work in, they'll fall behind those with more resilience.

The parable of the talents illustrates this concept well: the servants who invested their talents and grew them were rewarded, while the servant who buried his talent to preserve it, but not grow it, was exiled. We are to grow our talents. We do that through hard work. Resilience and hard work combined leads to performance, which is what drives our success.

If we're willing to follow Billie Jean King's wisdom and view pressure as a privilege, then we're going to be willing to rise to the occasion, be resilient, and perform at exceedingly high levels. If pressure is indeed a privilege, resilience the key to success, and willingness to endure part of performance, then we understand the equation of greatness.

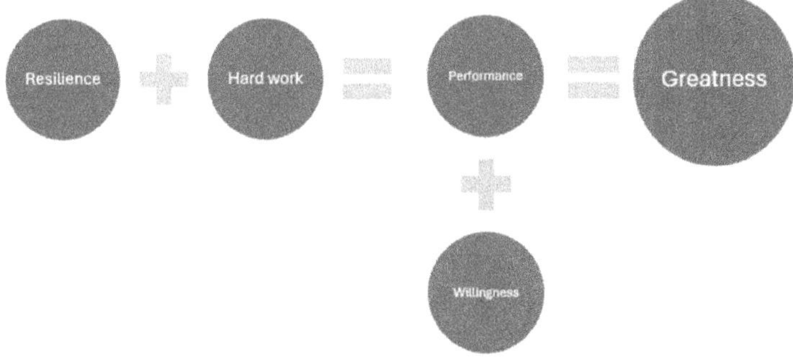

Six: Don't Drink Stagnant Water

I started this book with a story about hiking. I love hiking. I love being in the woods, reaching a vista, and being surrounded by nature. Someday I'm going to live in the mountains and have trailheads at my backdoor. There is little I find more rewarding than climbing to the top of a mountain and sitting and surveying this beautiful planet – at least the part of it I can see.

Loving something and being good at something, though, are two vastly different things. Real hikers would likely be appalled at me. My pace is slow. I use a backpack from Amazon and not some fancy outdoors retailer. I bring some essential survivor gear, like an emergency blanket, first aid kit, and paracord, but I don't have any extravagant ultra-lightweight equipment. I'm not through-hiking or backwoods camping; I'm just walking in the woods to see something beautiful.

The view is important to me. I live at sea level, which has its perks, but expansive vistas are not one of them. If I'm going to work hard and sweat and be physically challenged, I want the reward of a scenic outlook.

The story I opened this book with is completely true. I drove hours westward early in the morning, set up camp near the trailhead, changed my shoes and set off up the mountain. The trail was about 7.5 miles and designed in a loop that would take me to the top of the mountain where an outlook awaited. I calculated how much water I would need based on how long the hike would take me. What I failed to account for was the oncoming humidity.

When I started that hike the weather was pleasantly cool and a little cloudy. The forecast called for rain, but I had my rain jacket and a change of socks in my backpack. There is a motto that there is no bad weather, only poor planning, and I figured I had planned pretty well to endure a little rain.

The first part of that hike was beautiful. I was completely alone on the trail, walking through part of the forest that looked like a brush fire had swept through at some point. It was almost a ghost forest, with blackened trees and new fire growth. I was blissfully walking on my merry way when the rain started.

The rain came in quickly, as storms tend to do on mountains. Just before it started to pour, it was as though a cloud descended on where I was walking. Visibility dropped as I was suddenly transported into the middle of dense fog. With that cloud came humidity. Even with my rain jacket on, I was soaked within minutes. There isn't a way to escape getting wet when you're sweating under a jacket and the air you're walking through feels like the vapor cloud from a humidifier.

Even so, I thought it wasn't a big deal. Rain happens and fog passes; I just hoped the storm would clear by the time I got to the top. My wonderfully optimistic self, in that moment, didn't consider that I was losing a lot more water than I was taking in.

I passed a backcountry shelter that through hikers on the Appalachian trail used, which I thought was one of the coolest things I had ever done. Through hikers are a different kind of people, and while I don't think I'll complete the entire Appalachian trail, I love reading about those who do.

One of my favorite books is *Grandma Gatewood's Walk*. It's an amazing story of a woman, who after decades of horrific abuse at the hands of her husband, decided to walk the entire Appalachian trail. Emma Gatewood became the first woman to walk the entire trail, from Georgia to Maine, at age 67. She wore tennis shoes and sewed her own pack that she slung over her shoulder like a bag of flour. Her story was so inspiring to me, and I thought "If Emma can walk the entire trail, there is no reason I can't walk it in sections."

As I passed that shelter, soaking wet and a little miffed that my idyllic fantasy wasn't lining up with reality, I wondered if Emma Gatewood had slept there. She must have walked where I was walking, but I don't know when that shelter was built; it could have been long after she had passed through those same woods.

Part of me thought about stopping there and waiting out the storm. The reason I kept walking was the cold. Most people associate humidity with heat, which I understand living in a coastal area. Humidity can accompany any temperature, though, and that day it had not gotten any warmer than when I started. There was no way I was going to start a fire in that wooden shelter – being on the news as the idiot hiker that burned down an AT shelter was not on my agenda for the day.

At that point, I was sweating and soaked but if I took off my jacket, I would be uncomfortably chilled. I needed to keep it on and keep moving, because it's better to be warm and wet than cold and wet. So, I stared wistfully at that shelter, aware of all the amazing people who had done what I was doing, only multiplied by a thousand as they set their sights towards Maine.

Not far past that shelter I came to a signpost that was supposed to mark roughly the middle of the trail.

There were about 3.5 miles behind me, and four miles in front of me. This is where reality hit me like bus. I did not have enough water. I had not accounted for how much water I was losing through sweating under my jacket. I was thirsty, and I was looking at the bottles I had brought with the deep certainty they would not last me until I got back to the trailhead.

I don't want to make this sound more dramatic than it was. I wasn't in immediate danger of dying. There was a certainty, though, that I needed to keep moving to keep my core temperature up. Regardless of which way I turned from that signpost, I was going to be uncomfortable. I wouldn't shrivel up like a raisin in the sun and fall over from dehydration, but I didn't have the luxury of lollygagging, either. So, I needed to decide quickly about which direction I was going.

There was no helicopter coming to rescue me. A worm hole was not going to magically open and transport me to my car. It was a little maddening to be surrounded by water, but not in a way that was useful. Unless the rain pouring down around me suddenly funneled itself into a faucet-like stream, I couldn't utilize it.

It's tempting, when you're in the woods and looking for a water source, to find any puddle and drink it or dip your water bottle into it. Now again, I was not in immediate danger as long as I kept moving. It's not like I was Cheryl Strayed desperately seeking water on the Pacific Crest Trail, roasting in the desert, and tempted by animal troughs.

A little bit of thirst, though, is an interesting thing. Human brains are hardwired to seek water when thirsty. Scientists at the University of California studied the brain-body connection of thirst, trying to understand how our bodies communicate to our brains, and vice versa. The researchers found what they called "thirst neurons" in the brain that calculated if the body needed more water.

This is interesting because we know anecdotally that thirst elicits primal urges. It's easier to ignore your body's hunger cues than it is to ignore thirst. Another group of researchers found that mild dehydration can cause anxiety, which helps explain why humans have an intense need to seek out water.

How do we connect this to professional and personal development? Well, as I was trudging up that trail, having decided to walk upwards, I thought of what a perfect analogy my situation was for leadership. We are thirsty for information, knowledge, and growth. Leaders, or aspiring leaders, are looking for ways to quench that thirst, sometimes desperately. Being a leader can sometimes feel like walking up a mountain in wet socks with a limited water supply. It's anxiety inducing and uncomfortable.

It's tempting to drink from stagnant water. This is a survivalist no-no, as stagnant water is where bacteria proliferate. Drinking stagnant water is a good way to develop serious gastrointestinal distress – which will make dehydration worse. But surely, you say, drinking something is better than drinking nothing. I would tell you that mild dehydration is easy to recover from, while legionella and giardia are not.

The analogy here is that there will be people in life that are stagnant bodies of water. If we drink from them, we are taking a significant risk of making ourselves ill. So, what do stagnant water people look like? How can you tell if they're a safe source of quenching your thirst?

First, let's talk about what free flowing people look like. Free flowing people have psychological flexibility, which we've already talked about. Free flowing people are willing to adjust and pivot but are not reactive. They pursue their goals with quiet fierceness, just as rivers quietly and unrelentingly carve their way through solid rock. Free flowing people are refreshing to be around. They make us feel cool when we're enduring heat.

Leaders that willingly share knowledge and time are free flowing. Those that have resilience and tenacity, while maintaining their ability to be flexible, are flee flowing. Leaders that make you want to follow them are in the flow, and we want to join them as they travel towards the sea. These are the people we want to drink from. They nurture and grow us, so that we too may nurture and grow others. This is the kind of leader we need in our lives, and hopefully the leader we're working towards becoming.

Now that we know what flowing water looks like in a person, we can define what stagnant water looks like.

Stagnant water people are stuck in their ways. Just like the algae bloom in a little pond, they grow in ways that do not nurture or refresh us. They are maintain-the-status-quo at all costs people. They spread their biofilm of negativity, harshness, and discouragement to all people they meet.

We've all met the leader desperately clinging to the past, refusing to entertain the concept of change. That leader is stagnant. They are rejecting the incoming stream that may clear away the muck and slimy green growths in favor of maintaining the comfort of their little rock pool. Never mind that the rock pool is overgrown with toxic flora.

Rejecting change isn't the only symptom of stagnation. Refusing to share knowledge and mentor others is also a symptom. Leaders that are threatened by their star performers, or who hoard knowledge in the fear that others would surpass them in some way, are stagnant. Those leaders are stagnant pools filled with beavers, actively blocking all the incoming and outgoing streams while also dropping their giardia filled waste in the pool.

When we are looking for growth and mentoring, it's easy to get desperate. I have met leaders who were so thirsty for something new that they took roles they hated. They wanted to grow – they wanted opportunities – but in their haste, they jumped into a toxic, stagnant pool. I've been in situations where I was frantic to change jobs, and the temptation to take the first offer made to me, even when I knew it wasn't the right one, was intense.

When faced with those situations, it's helpful to remember that if we choose the wrong pool, it may take us a long time to recover. We were already thirsty, but now we're sick with an intestinal pathogen and losing fluids even more rapidly. Our thirst is only going to grow. I'm not cautioning you to wait for the perfect opportunity, or telling you to stay where you are, especially if you're in a stagnant pool already. But I would encourage you to seek out flowing water. Look for the job, or the leader, or the mentor, who will refresh you.

As leaders, we want to be flowing water people. If we're living with humility and psychological flexibility, then we will have radical openness and willingness to try and endure – and we will flow like a river. The next time you're in a challenging situation, sit and close your eyes and imagine a peaceful river. Imagine yourself as the water, flowing unrelentingly towards the sea, and then see what answers come to you. Adopt the mantra 'let it flow like a river,' and see where that mental exercise takes you.

SEVEN: EVERYTHING FOR A SEASON

I mentioned I started my leadership career in an organization I thought I would work for forever. In that organization, I met two mentors that would help shape me into the leader I am today. The first one was Sherry, who poured into me with a generosity of spirit I still think about today. The second person was Karen, who gave me my first chance to spread my wings and figure out what kind of leader I wanted to be.

I had been a supervisor for about 4 years when Karen offered me a position as manager in the utilization review department. She had seen me work on a system project and been impressed enough to call me and ask me to come talk to her about an opportunity. Excited for a new adventure, though I didn't yet know what it would entail, I showed up in her office ready to say 'yes' to whatever she offered me.

As the conversation progressed, she leaned forward and said, "This is going to be a playground for you."

I had no idea how right she was or how much she was offering. I walked into that department with no direct reports and no scope of practice. Karen told me to come in, get to know people, and then tell her where I thought I would fit.

It's difficult to convey the uniqueness of that experience. I had no responsibilities other than to do an assessment of the current state of affairs and tell Karen where I could help. Her statement that this would be a playground for me was spot-on. I had so much fun those first few weeks, it was difficult to contain my giddiness. I had to reel it in, because I could tell it was weirding people out.

I spent four years working for Karen, stretching my leadership wings, and figuring out what kind of leader I wanted to be. There was a plaque on Karen's wall, to the right of desk, which said 'what kind of legacy do you want to leave?' I thought about that a lot during those years, in between building processes and redesigning multiple departments.

It sounds like a dream, right? And for the first few years, it was. I forgot, though, that change in inevitable.

As I mentioned earlier in the book, 2020 was not a great year for me. This was the year my dreams of being a speaker and consultant seemingly died. It was the year I was scrambling to figure out how to be a leader for a remote team. And it was the year, with nothing left to challenge me and no big projects to work on, that I realized I was bored.

The change to working remotely was not one I took to gracefully. I was fully onboard with being remote, and I thought it made perfect sense in the context of the work my team did and what was happening in the wider world. Most of the people on my team were moms or grandparents, and with the schools and daycares closed, it was a struggle to work anywhere other than from home. The concept of remote working was one I understood and supported. The logistics of how to do it I did not immediately grasp.

The system I was working in at the time had a culture that relied heavily on in-person rounding. Leaders were supposed to round on their staff a minimum number of times per week, and we even had check in tools we were supposed to use. Building a relationship was predicated on how often you were having in-person meetings with your direct reports. This was a very 'be visible' culture.

There is nothing wrong with that culture. In fact, I really liked it and still believe that rounding is one of the best ways to support your on-site team. It does not, however, lend itself to an easy transition to fully remote work.

My supervisors were running the daily operations, and they were exceedingly competent. They did not need me on a day-to-day basis. (Managers, take note – that's a good thing). My team was mature enough they know their roles and didn't miss a beat when they started working from home. To top it off, census across the entire hospital system dropped as planned procedures were cancelled, so there was less work to do than usual.

This is when it hit me that I was ready for a change. I had probably been ready, hence my seeking out part time consulting and speaking work, but I wasn't ready to consciously acknowledge it was time for me to leave that organization. I started stalking the internal job board, but most hiring and promotions had been frozen. I felt stuck and anxious.

Leaving an organization you've been at for a long time is a scary decision. Learning a new role can be intimidating, not to mention the need to learn a new culture and set of expectations. I wondered where I could work, as I wasn't in a position to relocate my family. I was plagued with worries, like if I would find a role that would let me work remotely, or if I'd be able to find something I enjoyed.

I waffled on my decision to stay or go for longer than I should have. I wasn't disengaged, but I wasn't as exuberant as I had been for the prior few years. When we were told we had to return to work in a new location and a new office building, which I hated, the desire to find something new intensified. I was still putting all my career and emotional eggs in the basket of that company, though, so I kept looking on their job boards and nowhere else.

In our culture we tend to view things as valuable only when we perceive them to be permanent. We use phrases like "it's just a phase," to describe something new an adolescent is trying. We view hobbies we tried and then discarded as a waste of our resources or time. We celebrate longevity in companies.

The truth is, though, is that everything is a phase. Every part of our life is a phase. We are children, then adolescents, then adults, then seniors, and then we pass on. We enjoy things or activities for a period of time and then lose interest. We treasure friendships while we have them, but few are lifelong. Every aspect of our lives – be they personal or professional – is a phase. And every phase is valuable.

In mental health, some practitioners teach their depressed or anxious clients to disregard rules. If you liked photography a few years ago, but now you aren't interested and would prefer to crochet – start crocheting. Don't beat yourself up about quitting photography. If you have no energy to care for yourself and the thought of showering is exhausting, shower sitting or lying down. If you want to garden, but don't have the time to do so, nurture one potted plant. There really are no rules except the ones we place on ourselves.

That lesson about breaking free from arbitrary societal rules is partly based on the concept that all things, even those that are temporary, hold value. We're allowed to change hobbies. We're allowed to make new friends. We're allowed to change our style of dress or our hair or get a new tattoo. We can change our political leanings, how we manifest our spiritual beliefs, or if we believe there are aliens in the universe. Changing any of these things does not discredit our previous actions or beliefs. It is simply a sign we are growing.

I thought there was value in being a 'lifer' at my company. Karen had been there 35 years when she hired me, and I admired her for that. I thought staying power equated to my inherent value.

There is nothing wrong with staying at an organization for a long time, though I would argue it becomes more difficult to maintain perspective if you do so. What is wrong is being afraid to change because we believe it shows we failed or lack value. That's based on the concept of fairness and meritocracy – the concept that our company will promote us if we're good enough. But sometimes, for many reasons, that isn't the case.

There is a season for everything. There is a season to plant and a season to harvest. There is a season to develop new land. It was my season to learn new things, and it was time for me to grow somewhere else.

Another true motto is "you're not growing if you're not uncomfortable." Another version of that same motto is "you have to be comfortable being uncomfortable." I've heard those sayings a lot in my career, and as I was researching the origin of those quotes for this book, I found something interesting: a lot of people have said something to this effect, many of them successful leaders and entrepreneurs.

Peter McWilliams, a self-help author of almost forty books, is credited with saying "be willing to be uncomfortable. Be comfortable being uncomfortable." Alex Honnold, a spectacular free solo climber who has climbed some of the largest rock faces on the planet, has said "my comfort zone is like a little bubble around me, and I've pushed it in different directions and made it bigger and bigger…" Michael Phelps is quoted as saying "uncomfortable doesn't mean bad, uncomfortable simply means you're doing something you haven't done before."

Eleanor Roosevelt said, in 1960, "do one thing every day that scares you. Those small things that make us uncomfortable help us build courage to do the work we do." Sahil Lavingia, an entrepreneur, and founder of wildly successful Gumroad, said "Finding a new job is uncomfortable. Starting a company is uncomfortable. Learning a new skill is uncomfortable. Getting healthy is uncomfortable. Growth is uncomfortable."

The proliferation of this concept, going back decades, tells us there is truth here. I personally think discomfort leads to growth. At least, it has in my life. I've also seen the truth of discomfort equaling growth in the life of my clients. I'm honored to be a nurse practitioner, and I get to walk with clients on their journey to healing. That journey is inherently uncomfortable. Learning new thought habits, processing trauma, forgiving themselves for perceived failings – all very uncomfortable. But the clients who do that work transform into healthier and more balanced versions of themselves. It is the clients who are afraid of that discomfort who struggle to find healing.

If we believe that everything is for a season and everything is inherently transitory, then we must also accept that we will inevitably be uncomfortable. Things will change. Relationships will grow and contract and cease. Our jobs will fail to fulfill us. Our children will grow up and leave the nest. Our skin will wrinkle. If we're comfortable being uncomfortable, then we can appreciate the season we are in and approach the next season with radical openness and a willingness to grow.

I left my not-forever-company and dove into the madness of opening that substance use disorder treatment center with Chad. It was the most uncomfortable I had been in a decade, and it was the fastest period of my professional growth in years. There was a parallel relationship between my discomfort and my growth. I would not be the leader I am today if I hadn't tolerated that discomfort.

The belief in 'everything for a season' is a fundamentally important aspect of psychological flexibility, the importance of which we've already talked about. If we embrace change, tolerate discomfort, and are willing to continue to be open, we are on the path to living our best life.

EIGHT: LOVE YOUR TEAM

When I was a young leader, I conceptualized my role as the person who supported the team in reaching their goals. I thought the most important aspect of my role was as a subject matter expert in technical and managerial tasks. My interpretation of servant leadership was working to make the lives of my team members easier – better software, better training tools, hiring qualified people – that kind of thing.

It wasn't until after Sherry shared the harsh reality that my team didn't think I cared about them, and forced me to start saying good morning, that I started to understand leadership on a different level. The way I was conceptualizing leadership was more in line with the definition of management.

Management skills are crucial for those supervising teams. Teams cannot function without a good manager. Management skills are specific and necessary, but they are not the only skills needed to be a good leader.

Traditionally, I think we've thought about the difference between leadership and management using a Venn diagram like this one:

I don't think that's an entirely incorrect way of thinking about it, but it's too binary. Leadership and managerial skills are not different categories; management skills are a specific type of leadership skills. Here's a diagram to illustrate what I mean:

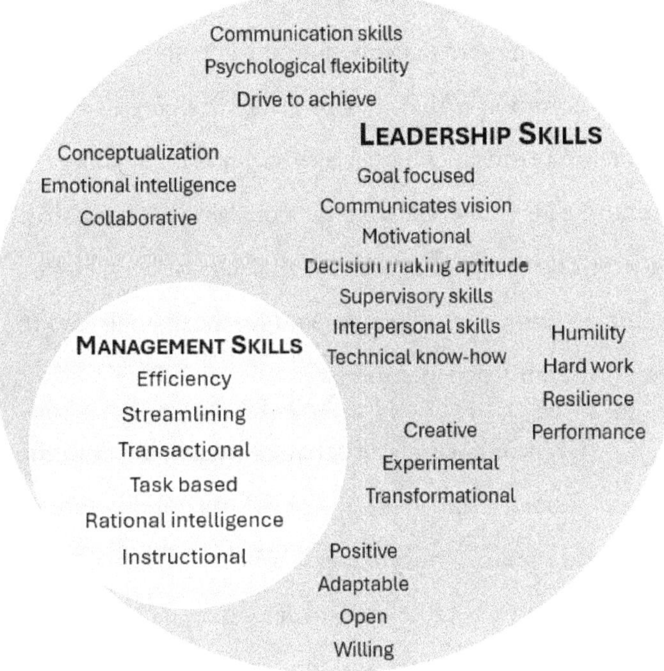

Leadership skills encompass management skills. This means that the best leaders have all these skills, and more. They can pivot between being transactional and inspiring; or use both rationale intelligence and creative intelligence. Managers need to be able to lead, and leaders need to be able to manage – though the focus and skill utilized most often may be different according to their roles.

So, what does this have to do with loving your team? Something management and leadership will always have in common is that they're difficult. Being in a leadership position, whether as a supervisor, manager, director, or CEO will always be a challenge. The reason leadership is difficult is because all layers of leaders are balancing company objectives and financial goals and the needs of their team members.

Everyone has a story. I am a firm believer in the power of stories, and I use analogies and parables a lot as a coach and mentor. Storytelling is a beloved human tradition. We've been telling stories since the dawn of humanity; it is an ancient and ingrained part of our makeup as a species.

I believe in stories partly because I acknowledge that I have many of my own, some of which I'm sharing in this book. I also believe that if I have this many stories, then everyone else must as well. How many of my team members are enduring personal hardship, financial stress, health concerns, or family issues? Those experiences, while the details are unique to the person, are ubiquitous to all people.

Let's acknowledge that all humans have stories, and all people endure challenges. Let's also acknowledge that all our team members, both direct and indirect, are humans. This means that all our team members are currently experiencing challenges in life. They may be small challenges, like a child who doesn't like their assigned lunch table, or they may be huge challenges, like a parent who was just diagnosed with cancer. Regardless of how we rate and weigh life events, we're all experiencing them.

So, how do we conduct ourselves knowing our people are human and experiencing human problems? Over the years, I've developed what I call a human-first approach. That's how I describe my leadership style these days. Human-first leadership is based on the concept of loving your team, which I know is a little woo-woo for a lot of leaders.

Founder and CEO Richard Branson's most famous quote is "take care of your employees and they'll take care of your business." The concept underlying this deceptively simple statement is that leaders need to treat their people as *people*.

My sister and I have a short-hand language we use with each other that often includes the statement "people are people," or something to that effect. She worked in the restaurant industry for a long time, and while her stories are her own, I will share that she encountered a wide range of people from myriad backgrounds. She would often opine that restaurant managers would forget they had human beings working for them and would say something along the lines of "[insert employee name here] just wants to be treated as a person."

That's a profound statement if we really think about it. I've used similar language with my kids when they have purposefully incited me to losing my marbles. "I'm a person, and I have feelings," is a statement not uncommon in my house and used to remind my children that while I am the monolith known as 'mom,' I'm also a person.

Being a person means we are experiencing the human condition: birth, emotion, learning, aspiration, dreaming, reasoning, conflict, and death. It's a vast and deep thing to conceptualize that every person on the planet is experiencing the condition of being a human, all the time, at every moment. It's a collective experience and it's what I mean when I say we're all people.

People want to be treated as though they matter. They want to be treated as though they have thoughts and opinions and feelings and trials and tribulations – because they do! If we are interacting with everyone on our team with the understanding that they are holistic and complex beings, and not a means to our own ends, we are using human-first leadership.

Some interactions are transactional, and that's normal. Even in transactional conversations, though, we're still speaking with another human. I think a good way to illustrate this is to point out the difference between how we speak to a computer program, like ChatGPT, and how we speak to each other.

I might type into ChatGPT something like "write me a speaker bio." I would certainly never talk to a person that way. I might reframe it if I was asking a person into "what would you include in a speaker bio?" That's the difference between having a process/outcome-first and a human-first approach.

Another way to conceptualize this approach is to describe it as loving your team. There is action associated with that. Love is an action in addition to a feeling. A common motto in my home growing up was "love is a verb." It was a statement meant to convey that love is an action word, like 'jump' or 'swing.'

Loving your team means genuinely wanting what is best for every person. It means speaking to them as people, and not automatons. It means making plans and goals with their best interest and experience at the forefront of our minds. Manifesting love at work looks different for every person and every environment, but for me it means showing compassion, having empathy and grace, and being generous.

I find it difficult to answer questions I deem ridiculous or be giving of my time if I don't love my team. Perhaps that's a character flaw, but I think all people have more grace and understanding towards those they love. I am not naturally generous with my time; it's the one thing I tend to hoard. I will freely share knowledge and resources, but I guard my time like a demented dragon on a pile of gold encrusted clocks. This is just an aspect of my personality, and I've come to understand and embrace it.

In order to be generous with my time, I need to love people. It's my nature to hiss and say 'no' and curl around my gilded pile when someone intrudes on time I had conceptualized of as mine. That is not the way to influence people and make friends, however, and people quickly realize when someone is stingy with their time. To relax my natural inclination and readily say 'yes' to demands on my time more often, I must hold love at the forefront of my mind.

Managers need to lead, leaders need to manage, and we all need to love our teams. These are interlocking and bidirectional circles, meaning all aspects of love, leadership skills, and management skills influence each other. In my mind, it looks something like this:

A leader that resents their team will never have a team that trusts them. A manager who thinks their team members are stupid will never be able to actively listen. Before we can expect people to follow us, we must first acknowledge and understand our inner landscape, including our beliefs and thoughts about other people.

Think about loving your team. Are you warm, generous, and understanding? Do you show genuine interest in them as human beings? Are you empathetic and compassionate? If those are words your team would use to describe you, congratulations! You have a team that will follow you to the ends of the Earth and go above and beyond to reach goals and improve outcomes.

If your team would describe you using the antonyms of those words, however, you may want to look at your metrics. Your metrics may help prove that a lack of love is hurting your business. If you're meeting your financial, growth, and marketing goals and you're a leader who doesn't love their team – you are one in a million (but not in a good way).

Love your team. Manifest that love in how to speak and interact with them. You may be surprised at the changes your team undergoes.

NINE: THE CHOICE BETWEEN SELF-AWARENESS AND IGNORANCE

The entirety of this book is predicated on the concept of self-awareness. I would argue self-awareness is the single most critical skill any leader can develop. Without self-awareness, we have no idea how we are perceived by others. Before we can understand our strengths and weaknesses and whether we love our team, we need to have the ability to be introspective.

Without self-awareness, we're left in a quagmire of navigating interpersonal dynamics while blindfolded and wearing noise cancelling headphones. We're like toddlers when they're in their most challenging phase – accidentally making a mess and unable to communicate clearly. Toddlers naturally grow out of that stage as they learn language and boundaries. Leaders without self-awareness, though, are perpetual two-year-olds.

As we've already established – leading is hard. It's hard not only because we are working with and managing people, who are all going through their own challenges and experiencing the human condition, but because leaders are accountable for goals. Leaders are taking their organization somewhere; to increased profits, greater market share, more brand recognition. Leaders are trying to accomplish something. Accomplishing great things will always be inherently difficult.

Leaders without self-awareness react to the pressure and pace of their roles with raised voices, attacks on their team members, and emotional lability. They are quick to anger, negative, and build relationships based on what people can give them, rather than what they can do for people. These leaders may have success (in some limited ways), but they will never have a legacy. They will never reach their ultimate goals, and will remain frustrated as they stay stuck, just out of arms reach of the finish line.

The real challenge with self-awareness is that people who tend to think of themselves as very self-aware are commonly the opposite. Large scale studies have found that only 10-15% of people are actually self-aware. That's a shockingly low number.

Self-awareness is the combination of two things: inner and external self-awareness. I relate this back to ACT, since that's the therapeutic modality I use the most often with clients. ACT is how we observe the self, which means our inner and outer worlds. We are individuals, of course, but we also exist in the larger universe, and thus must observe both.

Russ Harris, author and ACT trainer, defines ACT as "consciously bringing awareness to I-and-now experience, with openness, interest and receptiveness." That is also the ultimate definition of self-awareness.

Inner self-awareness is how we see our values, aspirations, thoughts, feelings, motivations, behaviors, and passions. It also encompasses how we view ourselves within our environment and how we view the impact we have on others. External self-awareness is the understanding of how other people experience us. The difference between these two concepts might be explained by thinking about the difference between sympathy and empathy. Sympathy is how we feel towards someone, while empathy is the ability to experience or understand how someone else feels. That is the nuanced difference between inner and external self-awareness.

Let's package the entire concept into this definition: having conscious awareness of our experience and the experience others have of us, with openness and receptiveness. People with high levels of self-awareness know who they are, what they want, and why they want it. They seek out and value the opinions of others. They incorporate feedback into their inner landscape and adjust their behavior accordingly. They are constantly striving for deeper understanding of themselves and those around them.

Conversely, people with low levels of self-awareness don't know what they stand for, how others perceive and experience them, or why they aren't accomplishing their goals. They externalize blame, rationalize failure, and may have unstable interpersonal and professional relationships. That all sounds pretty bad and it's unlikely anyone purposefully stives to be this person.

When I meet people who have low levels of self-awareness, I often notice a common theme. They lack humility. We spoke at length about humility already, and I won't belabor the point, but we cannot learn if we already think we know it all. The leaders I meet who would benefit from more self-awareness first need to work on their humility.

Humility is not the only foundational building block of self-awareness, though. The other critical component is psychological flexibility, which we've also already talked about. We must be both open to learning and willing to shift our perspective. Since I love diagrams, here is what this looks like, incorporated into our humility-connections diagram:

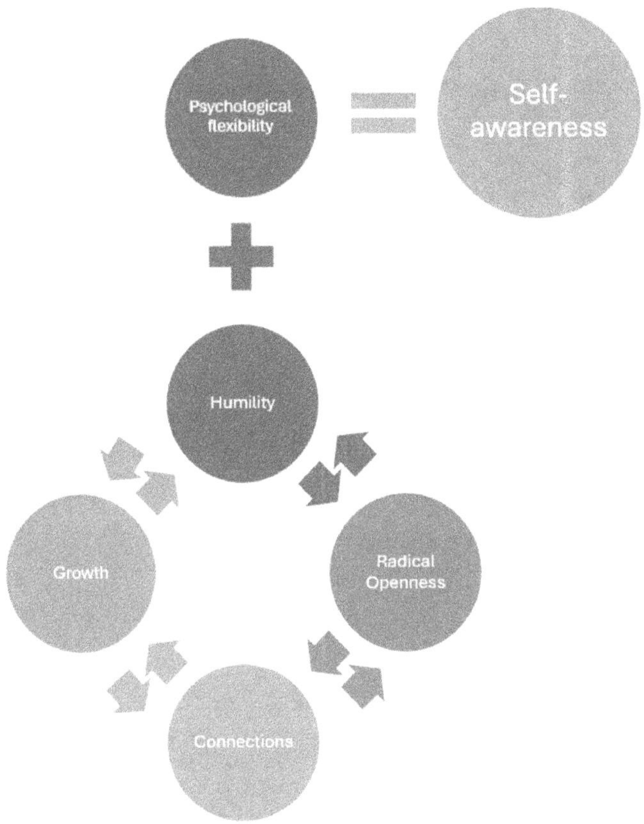

So, how do we pivot? How do we develop humility and psychological flexibility in order to gain greater self-awareness? A simple exercise may be practicing re-framing. Re-framing is simple in that anyone can do it, but difficult in that it requires practice. It's a skill that is simple, but not easy.

Reframing is a CBT technique. It is the practice of replacing one thought with a more helpful one. I like incorporating reframing into my practice and leadership, because it reminds me there is a different way to view something. Reframing opens us to the possibility that there are other perspectives, which can be freeing. If we release ourselves from definitives, what is left are possibilities, and that is inherently exciting.

Definitive statements are final. There is no room for change or improvement. They are like court rulings – binding, conclusive and unchangeable except through the lengthy legal process of appeals. Definitive thoughts are statements that we think are facts, like "I'm a good listener." That thought is an opinion, though there may be ample evidence to support it. Regardless of if the statement can be proven, it is definitive. There is no room for growth.

A re-frame of that same statement would be "I am always striving to be an active listener." That is a growth-oriented statement. It allows room for change. We may receive consistent feedback we are great listeners, but there is always room to keep growing. If we are humble enough to recognize we are still learning and growing, we'll be able to re-frame these definitive statements; in turn, reframing reminds us we are still works-in-progress, and therefore we should be humble – it's a positive feedback loop.

Here are some examples of reframing thoughts about ourselves:

Definitive	Growth Re-frame
I am a good listener.	I work to be an active listener.
I am a good leader.	I continually serve my team.
I am a good problem-solver.	I work to reach solutions.
I am creative.	
	I challenge myself to think outside the box.
I am self-aware.	
	I am gaining greater understanding of myself.

Notice there is a theme in these reframes of changing a statement of identity – "I am" – to a statement of action. Action implies movement, and we all want to be moving water. If we are reframing our definitive identity statements into growth-oriented statements, we're practicing humility, psychological flexibility, and avoiding stagnation. It's a win-win-win mental habit to develop.

I would argue the opposite of self-awareness is ignorance. I've had the experience of giving a leader feedback only to be met with a lack of composure and defensiveness. Those experiences were valuable, not only because they taught me what kind of leader I didn't want to be, but because they drove home the importance of self-awareness. A leader who reacts to feedback with defensiveness is a leader who is not yet self-aware.

No one wants to be ignorant. We should avoid being ignorant of ourselves more so than any other subject. We should be developing expertise on the topic of "us." That requires mindful observation of our inner lives and external world – which is, in a nutshell, self-awareness.

TEN: YOUR STORY IS YOUR OWN

Everyone has a story. We have a beginning, middle, and end to our lives. The beginning and end parts are relatively short, if we're blessed enough to lead long lives. The middle section is long. It's that middle section where we grow and learn and love and adapt.

It has been my experience that we love to tell other people about themselves. We try and tell people what their stories are. This isn't done out of malice – humans just like neat definitions, and groupings, and definitive statements. Leaders will give their employees feedback that sounds something like "you're good at data analysis," or "you're a people person." There may be evidence to back up those statements, but they are definitive statements about characteristics instead of feedback about behavior and performance.

I mentioned Sherry earlier in this book. She was my first mentor, and many lessons I learned from her stuck with me, and I will try to carry them for the rest of my career. I love her dearly and feel nothing but gratitude towards her. She wasn't always right about everything, though.

I remember once Sherry told me I was good with data, and alluded to that fact I was better with numbers than people. That was interesting to me because I don't actually like dealing with data that much. I use data every day, but I prefer to have an analyst compiling my reports for me – I like interpretation and application, not analytics.

It was not that nuance Sherry was speaking about, though. It was her perception of my people leading skills. At the time Sherry was my manager, I was going through certain events in my personal life that directly influenced how I treated myself and the people around me at work.

We are holistic human beings, after all, and it's impossible to bifurcate our personal and professional selves.

Sherry's perception was not wrong – at that time in my career, I did have more data and technical related skills than people skills. Her statement was wrong in that it was definitive. It was a statement of fact about who I was as a person, instead of my current skill set. I tell this story not in any way to reflect poorly about Sherry, but to make this point – people will tell you who you are; believe them only to a certain extent, because you are the author of your story.

I could have accepted that perception as fact and internalized my lack of people leadership skills. It would have made sense, given where I was mentally and what seemed like my natural talents at the time. But that would have precluded growth.

If you ask people I work with now, they would probably tell you I have far more people skills than data skills. Their perceptions are valid. In reality, I use both skillsets depending on the need at the time. We all have internal scales with different skills on them, and we re-balance those scales as situations change.

An example of this is parenthood. We tend not to treat our employees the way we treat our children. Hopefully, there is a core similarity in that we are being empathetic and supportive, but the messaging and delivery are probably quite different. That doesn't mean we're less able parents when we're speaking to our employees, or less able bosses when we're speaking to our children. We are just balancing the scales differently.

Let me reiterate: your story is your own. You may be in a position today that requires a high level of attention to detail, but you'd rather be working with big picture projects. You can have both skills, and rebalance your scales depending on the situation you are in. Each side of your scale may be a little differently weighted – I, for example, am more naturally inclined to the big picture, rather than the details – but just because one side is a little more natural doesn't mean the other side doesn't exist.

Listen to what people tell you. Take feedback. Remember, though, that we need to listen to the message not being spoken. Examine the intent or underlying perceptions behind the words – are we being praised for exhibiting a skill that was needed at a certain time? Are we being told how our boss perceives us, which we can use to determine what aspects of that perception we want to reinforce or change? Are we being told there is something within our portfolio of skills that needs additional development?

Ultimately, though, write your own story.

Steve Jobs was ousted from the company he founded. He went on to acquire Pixar and return to Apple as CEO, which led to Apple transforming into the powerhouse it is today. The first woman of color to be CEO of Xerox, Ursua Burns, grew up in relative poverty and obscurity. I'm sure people told her what her story was frequently in her life. She wrote her own story, though, and transformed Xerox, leading it into a new era. Steven Hawking was told his disease would limit him; he wrote some of the most important theories in physics, authored multiple best sellers, and is considered one of the greatest geniuses of our time.

There are countless other examples of people who changed the world because they believed they could write their own story. The limitations others placed on them were steppingstones to greatness.

These leaders also show us the power of resilience. As we discussed in chapter five, outcomes are the result of resilience plus hard work. The courage and fortitude to write your own story is also based on resilience and overcoming obstacles. Most people don't mean for their feedback to become an obstacle, but our human nature means we internalize beliefs based on what trusted advisors tell us.

If we tell our children they are messy and disorganized, they will be. If we tell our spouse they are unthoughtful, they will be. If we tell our employees they are only good at one thing, they will be. Instead of definitive statements, make room for growth. Re-frame the message so your audience can use your feedback as a rung on the ladder of self-improvement. In the same way, re-frame the messaging you receive to make it productive.

Write your own story.

PUTTING IT ALL TOGETHER

If we know and understand our values, we can build psychological flexibility. If we understand that everything is for a season, we will build psychological flexibility. Psychological flexibility plus humility will lead to willingness. Humility, radical openness, connections, and growth are all connected in a positive feedback cycle. Similarly, humility builds self-awareness, and vice versa.

Resilience and hard work lead to performance. Willingness and performance lead to outcomes. Willingness and preparation lead to readiness. Outcomes and readiness come together to yield greatness. The starting point for all those beautiful equations is love.

If you like diagrams (and are willing to squint), the entire picture looks like this:

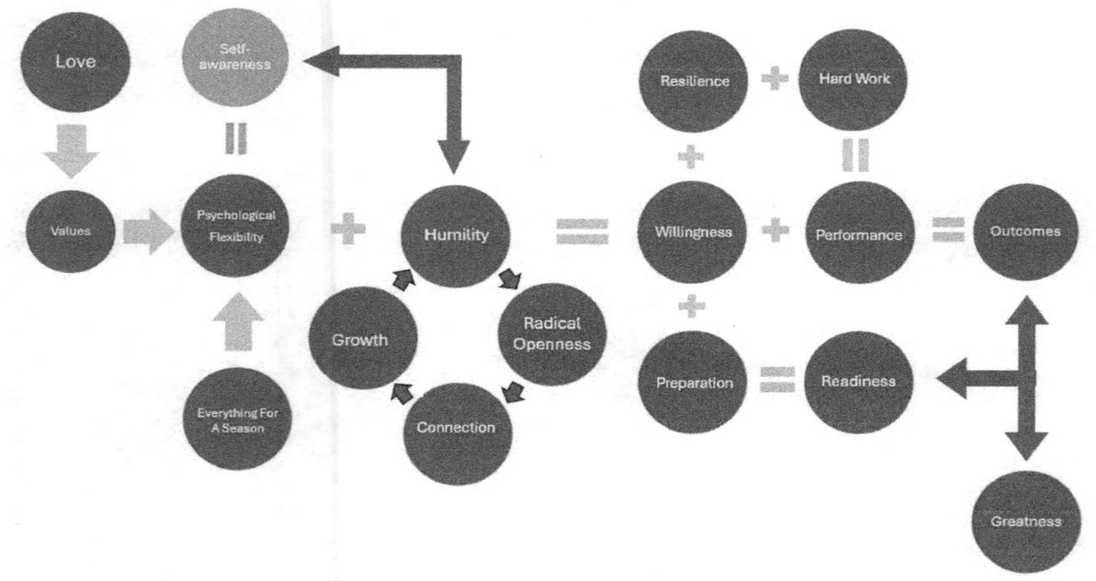

Love
Self-awareness
Values
Psychological Flexibility
Everything For A Season
Growth
Humility
Radical Openness
Connection
Resilience
Hard Work
Willingness
Performance
Outcomes
Preparation
Readiness
Greatness

I hope these lessons serve you well. I hope you take these stories and share them and then use them as templates to tell your own stories.

Speaking of stories, I'll finish the one I started this book with:

I did climb that mountain. I finished the 7.5-mile loop. Just as I reached the summit, the skies cleared. It was a beautiful view. I think of that hike frequently, and when I do, I am reminded that the best direction to go is upwards.

ABOUT THE AUTHOR

Dr. Tabitha Hapeman is founder of The Upwards Institute, a consulting firm specializing in leadership development, corporate culture, and healthcare revenue cycle solutions. Her background as a doctorate prepared nurse and psychiatric mental health nurse practitioner give her unique insight into the psychology of people and organizations. As a consultant and keynote speaker she works with companies to build their business, develop their people, and create positive cultures that attract and retain top talent.

To learn more about Dr. Hapeman and the services offered by her firm, visit www.UpwardsInstitute.com.